A JOURNEY WITH JONAH

To Ann Graham

Paul Murray OP

A Journey with Jonah

THE SPIRITUALITY OF BEWILDERMENT

the columba press

First published in 2002 by
the columba press
55A Spruce Avenue, Stillorgan Industrial Park,
Blackrock, Co Dublin
Reprinted 2003

Cover by Bill Bolger
Cover picture: 'Jonah escaping from the Whale', Codex Palatinus Latinus,
871, folio 16 recto © Biblioteca Apostolica Vaticana.
Origination by The Columba Press
Printed in Ireland by Betaprint, Dublin

ISBN 1 85607 363 7

Acknowledgements
The author wishes to thank the following for their encouragement and
practical assistance: Brian Lynch of The Columba Press, Robert Ombres OP,
Philip McShane OP, Jeremy Driscoll OSB, Kate and Louis Marcelin-Rice,
Luigina Orlandi, Josephine O'Connell OP and Breda Ennis.
The author and publisher gratefully acknowledge the permission of the fol-
lowing to use material in their copyright: 'All the Way Down' by Thomas
Merton, from *The Collected Poems of Thomas Merton,* copyright © 1977 by The
Trustees of the Merton Legacy Trust. Reprinted by permission of New
Directions Publishing Corporation and Pollinger Ltd; Biblioteca Apostolica
Vaticana for 'Jonah falling into the mouth of the whale', Codex Palatinus
Latinus 871, folio 15 recto; Edinburgh University Library for 'Jonah and the
Great Fish' by Rashid Al-Din (707AH, 1307AD), Ms Or 20, f 23v.
Scripture text from the New American Bible © 1970 by the Confraternity of
Christian Doctrine, Washington, DC. Used with permission. All Rights
Reserved.
Every effort has been made to trace copyright holders. If we have inadvert-
antly used copyright material without permission, we apologise and will
put it right in future editions.

Contents

Introduction   9

PART ONE
Obedience to the Word:
The Lesson of the Wild Storm   15

PART TWO
In the Belly of Paradox:
The Lesson of the Great Whale   29

PART THREE
Compassion without Limit:
The Lesson of the Wondrous Plant   47

The Book of Jonah   63

Introduction

One clear indication of the importance of the Book of Jonah is the fact that Jonah is the only ancient prophet with whom Jesus identifies himself in a dramatic way in the New Testament, and to whom he refers explicitly by name.[1] As soon, however, as we turn to read the book itself, with the thought of the book's importance in our minds, we find ourselves at once somewhat bewildered. For the so-called 'Book' turns out to be a text of only a few pages long; and Jonah, the prophet, a prophet of only one short sentence.

Even more surprising, Jonah is – sad to say – no hero. In fact, if anything, he's a sort of anti-hero. Normally we think of prophets as men of character. But, in this case, all that we can say of Jonah is that, in the Irish sense of the word, he's a *character*! I sometimes think the term 'Gubu factor' might almost have been coined to describe the extraordinary happenings in the story of this minor prophet. You remember what 'Gubu' stands for – GUBU: grotesque, unbelievable, bizarre

1. There are, in fact, three references made to Jonah in the New Testament: Matthew 12:38-42; 16:1-4, and Luke 11:29-32. On each occasion, Jesus speaks about what he calls 'the sign of Jonah'. Jesus also refers to Elijah the prophet on a number of occasions, but he identifies Elijah with John the Baptist not with himself.

and unprecedented.[2] And, let's face it, the text of the Book itself, with a cast of characters which includes thousands of animals in sackcloth and one great prophet-swallowing whale, might almost have been written, in another age, by the Irish comic genius, Myles Nagopeleen!

All that being said, however, I am convinced that the Book of Jonah is the most profoundly Christian of all the books in the Hebrew Bible, and the book from which we have most to learn at the beginning of this new millennium. What is more, given the book's great subtlety and, at times, quite pungent satire, I am myself persuaded that it is probably the most 'Irish' of all the books in the Bible!

But let's begin first with a brief outline of the story. The Book opens with Jonah rejecting God's explicit command to preach to the Gentiles of Nineveh. In fact, Jonah runs away as far as possible in the opposite direction, and gets on a ship bound for Tarshish. Soon, however, when a huge storm rises, the terrified men on the ship feel compelled to cast Jonah into the ocean. But, at that moment, a great fish – often pictured as a whale – swallows the astonished prophet.

2. These four words were used in a remarkable press conference given by the Irish politician, Charles J. Haughey, on 16 August 1982. According to one of Haughey's biographers, 'The press took up these dramatic words in reports and headlines, and out of the initial letters Conor Cruise O'Brien … constructed the acronym and mnemonic GUBU'. See Bruce Arnold, *Haughey: His Life and Unlucky Deeds* (London 1993) p.201.

Jonah remains inside the belly of the whale for three days, praying in his anguish, until he finds himself regurgitated unto land. Deciding, then, to obey God's command after all, he prophesies to the people of Nineveh the destruction of their city within forty days. The people of Nineveh repent, and God forgoes his threat of punishment against them. But this decision deeply irritates Jonah. He is all of a sudden filled with self-pity, and wants to die. His anger is further roused, when a plant, which had afforded him temporary shelter against the scorching heat, is withered. But somehow, by means of this incident, Jonah is brought to realise that God can show kindness to whom he will, no matter which race or nation the people belong to, and even if they are living within the evil city of Nineveh.

In outline, the story seems simple enough. In fact, the entire work consists of no more than forty-eight verses. And yet, around this small book, as if it were around Jonah's own troubled ship, high waves and storms of controversy have swirled for centuries. Vastly different currents of thought, represented by ancient rabbis and scholars, medieval and modern exegetes, contemporary believers and post-modern sceptics, have surrounded the work with questions concerning its date of composition, its authorship and literary genre, its basic theme and purpose. But so far, and perhaps not surprisingly, little or no consensus has been reached. In fact, at times, in terms of understanding, all we seem to have before us is what has been called by one exegete 'a tempest in a text'![3]

In some ways, the situation today is much as it was in the fourth century. At that time, St Jerome, in his own commentary on the Book, noted that although many Latin and Greek authors had already given their attention to The Book of Jonah, 'By their many questions they have not so much clarified as obscured the meaning, so much so in fact that their own interpretation needs itself to be interpreted, and the reader leaves more uncertain than he was before he began his reading.'[4] Twelve centuries later, Martin Luther levels a no less bitter complaint against St Jerome himself. Along with certain other fathers of the church, Jerome has obscured the text of Jonah, Luther claims, with 'intricate, innumerable, and silly questions', although the text itself is 'clear, easy to understand, and full of comfort'.[5]

---

3. Phyllis Trible, 'A Tempest in a Text: Ecological Soundings in the Book of Jonah', *Theology Digest*, Vol 43, 4 (Winter 1996) pp.303-12. On one key question, however, there is by now almost unanimous agreement among scholars, namely that the author of the Book of Jonah is not concerned with presenting a literal, historical account. 'Recognition of the book's literary qualities has turned the attention of interpreters to the work's character and function as story.' See 'Jonah' by A. R. Ceresko, in *The Jerome Biblical Commentary* (Englewood Cliffs, New Jersey 1990) p. 580.
4. St Jerome, 'Prologus', *In Jonam Prophetam*, P. L. 25, col 111.
5. 'Lecture on Jonah: The Latin Text, 1525', in *Luther's Works*, Vol 19, ed. H. C. Oswald (St Louis 1974) pp. 4-5.

In my own opinion some of the best commentaries on the Book of Jonah have not come from the scientific minds of exegetes, but from poems and paintings, sculpture, stained glass, childrens' stories and plays. These kinds of 'readings', when one work of art, or one 'construct of the imagination', responds to another – and responds from *within* the creative act or the creative process itself – are often, in George Steiner's opinion, 'of a penetrative authority rarely equalled by those offered from outside, by those propounded by the non-creator, that is to say the reviewer, the critic, the academic'.[6]

Undoubtedly, one of the most brilliant responses ever made to The Book of Jonah, is Herman Melville's *Moby Dick* and, in particular, the famous sermon delivered, in chapter nine, by the sailors' chaplain, Father Mapple. 'Shipmates,' the priest explains, 'this book [The Book of Jonah] ... is one of the smallest strands in the mighty cable of the scriptures. Yet what depths of the soul does Jonah's deep sea-line sound! What a pregnant lesson to us is this prophet!'[7]

---

6. George Steiner, *Real Presences* (Chicago 1989) p.12. For a reflection on some of the many different images of Jonah in art and literature, see James Limburg, 'Jonah and the Whale through the eyes of Artists' in *Bible Review*, Vol VI, 4 (August 1990) pp. 18-25. See also Yvonne Sherwood, *A Biblical Text and its Afterlives: The Survival of Jonah in Western Culture* (Cambridge 2000).
7. Herman Melville, *Moby Dick or The Whale* (London 1967) p. 47.

My intention here, in these pages, is to try to uncover something of the lesson, 'the pregnant lesson', of the prophet Jonah. But, as well as focusing attention on the text itself, I hope to take some soundings within the depths of the Jewish and Christian soul, to explore, that is, something of the impact Jonah has made, over the centuries, on the Judaeo-Christian tradition. But also, however briefly, I would like to note examples of the response which the Jonah story has awakened in a number of creative writers, poets, and artists, both inside and outside the Judaeo-Christian tradition.

The message of The Book of Jonah, its 'pregnant lesson', can I think be divided into three parts. Accordingly, the present study will be structured in a simple three-fold manner under the following headings:

1. Obedience to the Word: The Lesson of the Wild Storm
2. In the Belly of Paradox: The Lesson of the Great Whale
3. Compassion without Limit: The Lesson of the Wondrous Plant

PART ONE

Obedience to the Word:
The Lesson of the Wild Storm

'Arise and go to Niniveh'. These are words addressed uniquely to Jonah, requiring obedience. But, over the centuries, Jewish and Christian commentators and preachers and poets have, on occasion, extended the meaning of the text to include all of us in some sense. For now, or – if not now – sooner or later, all of us are called to go and face some 'Nineveh' of our own. There is a claim on us, on our time, on our love, on our courage, that we would rather avoid. In one of his *Divine Poems*, the seventeenth-century poet, Francis Quarles, describes the challenge to go to 'Nineveh' as a command, among other things, to do what justice demands. He writes:

> Jonah must go, nor is the charge confin'd
> To Jonah, but to all the World enjoyn'd:
> You magistrates, arise, and take delight
> In dealing Justice, and maintaining right:
> There lies your Nineveh; Merchants arise
> And mingle conscience with your Merchandise;
> Lawyers arise, make not your righteous Laws
> A trick for gain ...[8]

For Quarles, all the different vocations and professions are under the Word, under the call of God, even if here in his poem only three are mentioned explicitly: magistrates, merchants and lawyers. 'Merchant,' I suppose, must be a seventeenth-century name for what we'd call today a businessman

8. Francis Quarles, 'A Feast for Wormes: A Poeme of the History of Jonah', in *Complete Works in Prose and Verse*, Vol II (Edinburgh 1880) p. 10.

or woman. 'Merchants arise / And mingle conscience with your Merchandise'!

There is an interesting short play by Wolf Mankowitz – a twentieth-century play – in which Jonah appears as a sort of travelling salesman 'who has his eye out for a sharp bargain', but who finds himself all of a sudden called to be a prophet.[9] The call does not please this twentieth-century Jonah one little bit. He cries out at one stage in the play: 'You can't do this to me. I am on very important business'![10] And, in another place, he exclaims: 'Please, please, what do you want from my life? ... All these years I've been running – a traveller – Jonah, the traveller, representing Top Hat; Braces For The Trousers; Fair Lady Fancy Buttons; Hold Tight Hair Grips – only good brands in the suitcase. Ask them in Tarshish ... I shouldn't have to run with a suitcase any more. And still he nags me. All right. I heard. I'm going.'[11] To Jonah's profound irritation, the voice of God always comes to him, throughout the play, in the form of birds chirping inside his head. 'I hate birds,' Jonah complains. And then: 'You know what it says? "Arise, Jonah, arise. Go to Nineveh, that great city, and cry against it." I ask you. Why pick on me?'[12]

---

9. Wolf Mankowitz, *It Should Happen to a Dog: A Play in One Act,* in *Religious Drama* 3, ed. P. Smith (Glouchester, Mass. 1972) p. 123.
10. *Ibid.,* p. 129.
11. *Ibid.,* p. 125.
12. *Ibid.,* p. 126.

The humour in Mankowitz's play echoes the humour in the Book of Jonah itself. But the message about obedience remains a serious one all the same. And it occurs to me that, perhaps in all of the literature about Jonah, no one keeps the seriousness of this message more to the forefront of his mind than Father Mapple in *Moby Dick*. 'As with all sinners among men,' the priest declares, 'the sin of this son of Amittai was in his willful disobedience of the command of God – never mind now what that command was, or how conveyed – which he found a hard command. But all the things that God would have us do are hard for us to do – remember that – and hence, he oftener commands us than endeavours to persuade. And if we obey God, we must disobey ourselves; and it is in this disobeying ourselves wherein the hardness of obeying God consists.'[13]

Father Mapple paints a vivid picture of Jonah skulking about the wharves of Joppa, hiding from God, and seeking 'a ship that's bound for Tarshish':

Miserable man! Oh! Most contemptible and worthy of all scorn; with slouched hat and guilty eye, skulking from his God; prowling among the shipping like a vile burglar hastening to cross the seas. So disordered, self-condemning is his look, that had there been policemen in those days, Jonah, on the mere suspicion of something wrong,

13. *Moby Dick*, pp. 47-8.

had been arrested ere he touched a deck … in vain he tries to look all ease and confidence; in vain essays his wretched smile.[14]

Of course, in the end, Jonah does manage to get on board a ship. But very quickly he goes down into the hold of the ship, and is soon fast asleep. But then, all of a sudden, as if in imitation of the prophet's disobedience, 'the sea rebels'.[15] In Father Mapple's words: 'A dreadful storm comes on, the ship is like to break. But now when the boatswain calls on all hands to lighten her; when boxes, bales, and jars are clattering overboard; when the wind is shrieking, and the men are yelling, and every plank thunders with trampling feet right over Jonah's head; in all this raging tumult, Jonah sleeps his hideous sleep'.[16]

The text of The Book of Jonah itself reads: 'Then the mariners became frightened and each one cried to his god … Meanwhile, Jonah had gone down into the hold of the ship, and lay there fast asleep. The captain came to him and said, "What are you doing asleep? Rise up, call upon your God! Perhaps God will be mindful of us so that we may not perish".' (Jonah 1:6) The anguish of the captain brings to mind at once the anguished cries of the disciples of Jesus, in St Mark's

14. *Ibid.*, p. 48.
15. *Ibid.*, p. 50.
16. *Ibid.*, p. 51.

gospel, during a comparable storm. In chapter four, we read: 'the waves beat into the boat, so that the boat was already filling. But he was in the stern asleep on the cushion; and they woke him and said to him, "Teacher, do you not care if we perish?".' (Mk 4:37-8) Almost like a new Jonah, Jesus would seem to have found himself here in the same situation as the bewildered son of Amittai. But, in spite of the marked similarities between these two incidents, there exists of course an enormous gap between the state of mind of Jesus and that of our unhappy prophet.

St Jerome, commenting on this particular passage, and wanting Jonah to be a hero, not a coward, attributes Jonah's sleep to what he calls 'the serenity of the soul of the prophet'.[17] Jerome asserts that Jonah is calm even in the face of imminent shipwreck, since 'neither tempest nor dangers disturb him'.[18] The suggestion, though greatly complimentary to the prophet, is clearly untenable. And even St Jerome appears to change his mind within the space of a paragraph, openly acknowledging the fact that Jonah knows very well that the tempest is actually 'raging against him', and against no-one else. *That*, Jerome says, is the real reason why Jonah goes down into the hold of the ship, and seeks oblivion in sleep. So intense are his feelings of sadness and guilt, he simply cannot bear, it seems, the pain of staying awake.

17. *In Jonam Prophetam*, col 1125.
18. *Ibid*.

Reflecting on this particular stage in the story, Father Mapple, in *Moby Dick*, draws a sharp comparison between Jonah's condition and that of an unhappy drunkard: 'Like one who after a night of drunken revelry hies to his bed, still reeling, but with conscience yet pricking him … at last, amid the whirl of woe [which he is feeling], a deep stupor steals over him, as over the man who bleeds to death, for conscience is the wound, and there's naught to staunch it; so, after sore wrestling in his berth, Jonah's prodigy of ponderous misery drags him drowning down to sleep.'[19]

The understandable but desperate strategy of sinking down, as far as possible, into the stupor of sleep is, of course, simply a way of refusing to hear the voice of God, refusing to obey. I think it is no accident of grammar that our English word 'disobedience' comes from the Latin *'obaudire'* (to listen), and so *dis*-obedience, then, means literally 'not to listen'. Jonah's impulse to avoid responsibility and evade the command of destiny, by hiding himself away in the womb of sleep, has inevitably attracted the attention of many modern psychologists. For them the story of Jonah is 'not only a religious manifesto; it is also a psychological tableau of the human condition'.[20] The 'Jonah' in *us*, we are told, desires somehow to regress back into the warm, protective womb of

19. *Moby Dick*, p. 50.
20. See André Lacoque and Pierre-Emmanuel Lacoque, *Jonah: A Psycho-Religious Approach to the Prophet* (Colombia 1990) p. 217.

the mother. In his book, *The Forgotten Language*, Eric Fromm suggests that the images of 'going into the ship, going into the ship's belly, falling asleep, being in the ocean and being in the fish's belly' are all 'symbols' which stand for 'a condition of being protected and isolated, of safe withdrawal from communication with other human beings'.[21]

This solipsistic tendency on the part of Jonah – what psychologists refer to as 'the Jonah-and-the-whale complex' or 'the Jonah syndrome' – is, we are asked to believe, a tendency that forms part of the 'Jonah' make-up within all of us. I have no doubt that there is wisdom in this theory.[22] But what interests me here are not so much the psychological manifestations of this tendency, but rather the complex form that it has assumed today in contemporary spirituality. As all of us are well aware by now, there is a new fascination among our contemporaries with the things of the spirit. Unfortunately, however, that interest doesn't always translate into a capacity to attend to the living voice of God, or surrender with faith and hope and love to the transcendent beauty and pressure of divine revelation. Instead, there is a tendency to live one's spirituality within the bubble of the self, and practice what

21. Eric Fromm, *The Forgotten Language* (New York 1951) p. 22.
22. Carl Gustav Jung was the first to use the term, 'Jonah-and-the-Whale complex'. See Jung, *Symbols of Transformation*, trans. R. F. C. Hull (New York 1956) p. 419.

Martin Buber has called, in a memorable phrase, 'the religion of pure psychic immanence'.[23]

Modern consciousness, Buber writes, looks to the soul as the *only* sphere in which we can expect to harbour or discover the 'divine'.[24] And this marks, of course, a complete shift away from transcendence to immanence. In Buber's opinion, '[Modern consciousness] will have nothing more to do with the God believed in by the religions, who is to be sure present to the soul, who reveals himself to it, communicates with it, but remains transcendent to it in his being'.[25] A spirituality of this kind – an exclusively *immanent* spirituality – at least in its extreme manifestations, represents a regress back to a safe, controlled environment, a return to 'the womb' even. In terms of religion, it is nothing less than a spiritual manifestation of 'the Jonah syndrome'.

But let us turn our attention back once more to the text itself: Chapter 1, verses five and six. 'Jonah had gone down into the hold of the ship, and lay there fast asleep. The captain came to him and said, "What are you doing asleep? Rise up, call upon your God! Perhaps God will be mindful of us so that we may not perish".' A moment ago, I attempted, and in a

23. Martin Buber, *Eclipse of God: Studies in the Relation between Religion and Philosophy* (New York 1957) p. 84.
24. *Ibid.*, p. 83.
25. *Ibid.*

none-too-complimentary fashion, to relate Jonah's sleep to certain forms of contemporary spirituality. But, thinking further about Jonah's sleep, I cannot escape the thought that the thrust and challenge of this text relate, whether we like it or not, to those among us who consider ourselves members of Christ's church, and in particular to those of us who feel called to be preachers of the Word. For, like Jonah, we have been given a task to complete, and a message to preach to the world, but are we preaching it? Are we not, perhaps, living in a kind of bubble ourselves?

'The church today is in retreat.' This bald, simple statement was included in a sermon about Jonah, which was preached at Westminster Chapel, London, some years ago. But it is a sermon that could, I think, be preached again today. The church, though entrusted with the Word of truth is, we are told, like Jonah, because it 'has looked to Tarshish and not Nineveh. The church is like Jonah who paid the fare to sail on the ship going in the opposite direction from what God had demanded. The church has spent its energy, its time and its money on the wrong things. The church at the present time is like Jonah, asleep in the sides of the ship while the world is tossed in unprecedented bewilderment. The world is afraid – the church is asleep. The world asks questions – the church has no answers.'[26]

---

26. R. T. Kendall, *Jonah: Sermons Preached at Westminster Chapel* (London 1978) p. 11.

When, finally, Jonah emerges on deck, he finds himself forced to admit that he is the cause of all the trouble, and that he should, therefore, be thrown overboard at once. 'It is because of me,' he says to the sailors, 'that this violent storm has come upon you.' (Jonah 1:12) In a lengthy Latin poem, *Carmen de Jona et Ninive*, which for centuries had been attributed to Tertullian, Jonah is heard to exclaim – and the phrase I think is remarkable – 'In me is the storm. I am all the madness of the world'. *[E]go tempestas, ego tota insania mundi.*[27] In the next verse of the poem, Jonah is heard to cry out: 'It is in me / That the sea rises, and the upper air / Down rushes; land in me is far, death near, / And hope in God is none.'[28]

In spite of Jonah's despair at himself, the sailors, according to The Book of Jonah, try their best to control the storm. They make a last, desperate effort to get Jonah and themselves safely back to land. But the sea becomes ever more turbulent. The reality of Jonah's disobedience has to be faced, and the consequences accepted. The sailors take up Jonah in their arms, and throw him into the deep.

27. 'Carmen de Jona et Ninive', 1112, *Tertulliani Opera Omnia*, Tomus Posterior (Paris 1866) PL II, col 1170.

28. 'A Strain of Jonah the Prophet' [Carmen de Jona et Ninive] trans., S. Thelwall: 'Appendix' in *Tertullian, The Ante-Nicene Fathers, Vol IV*, eds. A. Roberts and J. Donaldson (Edinburgh 1885) p. 128. Martin Luther, in his commentary on Jonah, notes that 'a much greater storm was raging in Jonah's heart and conscience than raged on the sea outside'. 'Lecture on Jonah: The Latin Text', p. 10.

One early Christian author, who identified himself, in a particular way, with this moment in the life of Jonah, was an Irish saint. His name, in its original form, meant 'dove'. And that, as it happens, was also the meaning, in Hebrew, of the name 'Jonah'. The saint in question is, of course, none other than the remarkable Abbot of Luxeuil and Bobbio, St Columban. In 610 Columban found himself expelled from Burgandy, after he had spoken out against the wild sexual mores and pagan life-style of Theodoric II. In 613, writing in a letter to Pope Boniface IV, Columban dares to compare himself with Jonah since, just a few years earlier, with the threat of expulsion hanging over his head, he had come very near to experiencing the 'shipwreck' of all his hopes.[29] On another occasion, finding himself in the midst of an ecclesial storm, which had been brewing for many years, Columban wrote to one particular group of bishops who were involved in the controversy, and who were decidedly opposed to his way of thinking, and acting: 'If on my account this storm is upon you, take me and cast me into the sea, that this tempest may recede from you in calm; yet let it first be your part, like those mariners [in the Book of Jonah], to seek to save the shipwrecked by the bowels of godliness, and to draw the ship to land'.[30]

---

29. 'Letter V', 16, in *Sancti Columbani Opera*, ed. G. S. M. Walker (Dublin 1997) p. 55.
30. 'Letter II', 7, p. 19.

In Letter IV – undoubtedly the most moving of all the letters of Columban – the famous Abbot writes to his own religious brethren, and asks his 'frugal brothers'[31] to pray for his safety. Referring to himself as a 'sinful dove' (*colomba peccator*),[32] he draws their attention to the great drama and vulnerability of his present situation by suggesting an identification with the prophet Jonah at the moment of his expulsion into the deep. He writes: 'If I am cast into the sea like Jonah, who himself is also called Columba in Hebrew, pray that someone, a safe concealor, may take the place of the blessed whale, and by rowing, restore me, your Jonah, to the land he longs for.'[33] The passage, though brief, is so distinctive in its expression, and so poignant in its meaning, it impresses me as nothing less than a sharp, bright jewel in St Columban's writing. Nevertheless, the episode of the whale – as the saint remembers it here – the episode in the Jonah story which we are

---

31. 'Letter IV', 1, p. 27.

32. *Ibid.*

33. 'Letter IV', 8. The image of the whale appears again in a story concerning another famous Irish saint, also called Columba, or sometimes Colmcille. In an early life of the saint, in one section, we read of 'How the saint spoke with foreknowledge concerning a great whale'. Apparently, a brother in the community, named Berach, when he was about to set out on a journey by boat, was told by St Columba that he would confront on the open sea 'a prodigious monster'. And, in fact, Berach and his sailors did see 'a whale, of marvellous and enormous size, swimming on the surface', and 'it rose up like a mountain, and opened gaping jaws, with many teeth'. See *Adomnan's Life of Columba*, ed. A. O. Anderson and M. O. Anderson (London 1961) pp. 245-47.

about to examine next is, to say the least, somewhat glamorised, and the whale itself practically canonised! For what actually awaits the prophet Jonah, after he finds himself cast out of the boat by the sailors, is – as we will discover in a moment – by no means an easeful trip home!

PART TWO

In the Belly of Paradox:
The Lesson of the Great Whale

'Just as Jonah spent three days and three nights in the belly of the whale, so will the Son of Man spend three days and three nights in the bowels of the earth.' In this passage, from chapter twelve of St Matthew's gospel, Jesus compares himself to Jonah, and he refers explicitly to a 'whale'. The Book of Jonah itself, however, speaks only of 'a large fish': 'The LORD sent a large fish that swallowed Jonah; and he remained in the belly of the fish three days and three nights.' (Jonah 2:1) A short statement, laconic almost to a fault, but it has captured the imagination of countless generations of believers, both Jewish and Christian. Here is a passage, for example, from a Jewish work of the ninth century concerning Jonah and the fish. It is a prose work, but at times it reads almost like a poem: 'Rabbi Tarphon said: "That fish was specially appointed from the six days of Creation to swallow up Jonah ... He entered its mouth just as a man enters the great synagogue, and he stood (therein). The two eyes of the fish were like windows of glass giving light to Jonah".'[34]

The idea of a light somehow illuminating the insides of the fish was also put forward by another rabbi in the same text, but the form of light suggested was something entirely different: 'Rabbi Meir said: "One pearl was suspended inside the belly of the fish, and it gave illumination to Jonah, and it showed to Jonah all that was in the sea, and in the depths".'[35]

34. *Pirkê de Rabbi Eliezer* [The Chapters of Rabbi Eliezer the Great] trans. G. Friedlander (New York 1971) p. 69.
35. *Ibid.*, pp. 69-70.

I think it's worth noting here that, in the literature of the ancient world (whether in the form of myth or story), the image of an enormous fish alive in the ocean – a primeval sea-monster – occurs over and over again. And, what is more, the possibility of such a creature existing has continued to fascinate people even up to modern times. Leonardi da Vinci, for example, while engaged in developing a theory about the growth of the earth, and pondering in particular the significance of certain bones which he thought might have belonged to a primeval sea-creature, suddenly turned upside-down the page on which he was working, and addressed the putative, god-like creature in these words: 'O how many times were you seen among the waves of the great swollen ocean, with your black and bristly back, looming like a mountain, and with grave and stately bearing!'[36]

Among the Christian commentators on Jonah, one of the most interesting and original is Martin Luther. Here, with characteristic verve, is Luther pondering the mystery of Jonah's experience inside the whale: 'It must have seemed an interminably long time that he sat there in the dark. Yes, I suppose that he occasionally lay down and stood up ... How often lung and liver must have pained him! How strange his abode must have been among the intestines and the huge

36. Folio 265 of the *Codex Atlanticus*. Cited in Italo Calvino, *Six Memos for the Next Millenium*, trans. P. Creagh (New York 1988) p. 79.

ribs!'[37] Jonah's mysterious suffering inside the whale, and his sudden, unexpected release three days later, comprise a story, an image, that is referred to and reflected on over and over again by many of the great Christian commentators. St Augustine of Hippo, for example, towards the end of his life, remarked: 'Jonah prophesied Christ rather in suffering than in speaking, and that most manifestly in regard to the passion and resurrection. For why was he three days in the whale's belly and then let out, but to signify Christ's resurrection from the depth of hell on the third day?'[38]

Although there are a number of texts written by the early Christian fathers on the subject of Christ as the new Jonah, it was not on parchment, but on stone – in coloured fresco, in fact – that we find the first extended Christian testimony or presentation of Jonah as the image of Christ. Those pilgrims or tourists who have had the opportunity to visit the catacombs in Rome, will no doubt have been surprised at how often the early Christians painted the image of Jonah on the walls. Louis Réau, in his work *Iconographie de l'art chrétien*,

---

37. Martin Luther, 'Lecture on Jonah : The German Text, 1526', *Luther's Works*, Vol XIX, ed. H. C. Oswald (St Louis 1974) p. 68. Worth comparing and contrasting with Luther's imaginative rendering of the text is the playful but sardonic commentary by Voltaire on the brief, unhappy sojourn of the prophet inside the whale's belly. See Voltaire, 'Les questions de Zapata' (1767) in *Voltaire: Mélanges* (Paris 1961) p. 960.
38. St Augustine, *De Civitate Dei*, Bk 18, 30. See *Corpus Christianorum*, Vol XLVIII, p. 621.

even goes so far as to suggest that the image of Jonah arriving safely on shore after being ejected by the whale, is 'the essential image' for the early Christians.[39] And why? Because it is an image that reveals, with great vividness, to the many Christian men and women undergoing persecution at the time, the hope of a sure resurrection, and the promise of life eternal.

Jonah's exit from the whale – in the tradition of early Christian art in Ireland – was also understood as a symbol of the resurrection, and was represented in both bronze and stone. One of the most interesting examples is the Irish crozier-head found at Aghadoe (Kerry). The stem of the crozier curves at the top, and becomes a small Jonah valiantly making his exit from the open jaws of the whale, 'dressed like an acrobat in a tight-fitting jersey'.[40]

Jonah's whale also makes a somewhat dramatic appearance in at least one of the mystery plays – *'sacre representazioni'* – which were produced annually by a company of young tradesmen attached to the Dominican Priory of San Marco in

---

39. Louis Réau, *Iconographie de l'art chrétien*, Vol II, Ancien Testament (Paris 1956) p. 417.
40. See Françoise Henry, *Irish Art in the Romanesque Period: 1020-1170 A.D.* (London 1970) p. 114; Pl. 85, Fig. 9. For examples of stone carvings of Jonah in Ireland, see F. Henry, *Irish Art in the Early Christian Period (to 800 A.D.)* (London 1965) pp. 128, 130, 147, 156.

Renaissance Florence. Documents in the Magliabechi collection of the National Library in Florence indicate that the young company spent almost all its income on the stage properties and costumes they thought necessary for each individual performance. The treasurer of the company in 1449 was more than a little irritated, it would seem, when, for one particular performance, an enormous amount of money was spent on a great whale made out of paper and wickerwork, and decorated all over with gold stars. In the play, which was performed on the feast of the purification, Jonah, taking his turn with the other prophets from the Hebrew Bible, was summoned forward by an angel to declare his fore-knowledge of Christ the Son of God. Emerging, then, we may presume, from the belly of the great paper-whale itself, Jonah would be heard to exclaim:

> Three days I remained in that sea-fish,
> A symbol of forgiveness of sins,
> for that's how long Christ remained in his tomb
> and then triumphed with his human nature.[41]

In the Book of Jonah, chapter two, before God commands the

---

41. See *Rappresentazione della Purificazione*, Vol II, 177-80, in Nerida Newbigin (ed.) *Nuovo corpus di sacre rappresentazioni Fiorentine del Quattrecento* (Bologna 1983) p. 95. See also N. Newbigin, 'The *Rappresentazioni* of Mysteries and Miracles in Fifteenth-Century Florence', in T. Verdon and J. Henderson (eds.) *Christianity and the Renaissance: Image and Religious Imagination in the Quattrocento* (New York 1990) pp. 361-75.

fish to spew his captive out unto the shore, Jonah, we are told, from inside the belly of the great fish, prays 'to the LORD his God'. (Jonah 2:2) The prayer or psalm is an impressive canticle of praise. But it is also deeply moving in the way it reveals the terror and distress of the stricken prophet.

> The waters swirled about me, threatening my life;
> the abyss enveloped me;
> seaweed clung about my head.
> Down I went to the roots of the mountains;
> the bars of the nether world
> were closing behind me forever. (Jonah 2:5-6)

It is not difficult to imagine how both Jewish and Christian communities, undergoing great persecution, would at once identify with the hope and anguish of the drowning Jonah. An anonymous poet from the Jewish tradition, for example, a poet of no pretension whatever, wrote these stark few lines:

> Jonah prayed to the Lord:
> And to Him I appeal in my trouble;
> To the Lord I plead from Sheol's belly,
> You hear my voice.
> I gaze upon your holy shrine.
> You raise me from the grave alive.[42]

---

42. The original Hebrew text is published in Peter Schäfer, *Synopse zur Hekhalot-Literatur* (Tübingen 1981) pp. 144-45, cited in Jack Sasson, *Jonah* (New York 1990) p. 215.

Jonah's going down into the depths of the ocean has been understood as a descent into death, a descent into the very pit of hell itself. Again, no one, I think, has ever described this journey better than Herman Melville. The passage I have in mind is again taken from *Moby Dick*, and from the sermon of Father Mapple:

> God came upon him in the whale, and swallowed him down to the living gulfs of doom, and with swift slantings tore him along 'into the midst of the seas', where the eddying depths sucked him ten thousand fathoms down, and 'the weeds were wrapped about his head', and all the watery world of woe bowled over him. Yet even then beyond the reach of any plummet – 'out of the belly of hell' – when the whale grounded upon the ocean's utmost bones, even then, God heard the engulphed, repenting prophet when he cried. Then God spake unto the fish; and from the shuddering cold and blackness of the sea, the whale came breeching up towards the warm and pleasant sun, and all the delights of air and earth; and 'vomited out Jonah upon the dry land'.[43]

That last image of Jonah being 'vomited out upon the dry land' caught the attention of quite a number of well-known writers and poets in the twentieth century. Hart Crane, for example, in a tongue-in cheek poem entitled, 'After Jonah',

43. *Moby Dick*, p. 53.

recounts how, out of the 'snare' of the whale's belly, the poor prophet was 'belched back like a word to grace us all'.[44]

Thomas Merton, the American Trappist monk, also composed a poem on the subject. It's a great poem, I think, but it's not a pious poem. And maybe that's the reason why, during Merton's own life-time, it was never included in one of his many collections of poems. The work, entitled 'All the Way Down (Jonas, Ch. 2)', evokes rather vividly the image of the prophet. But the voice Merton lends to Jonah, or rather lends to what one might call the Jonah within himself, is that of a brilliant, uncontainable, feisty and exuberant, self-willed and cantankerous monk!

All The Way Down (Jonas Ch. 2)

I went down
Into the cavern
All the way down
To the bottom of the sea.
I went down lower
Than Jonas and the whale.
No one ever got so far down
As me.

44. Hart Crane, 'After Jonah', in D. Curzon (ed.) *Modern Poems on the Bible: An Anthology* (Philadelphia 1994) p. 336.

I went down lower
Than any diamond mine
Deeper than the lowest hole
In Kimberly
All the way down
I thought I was the devil
He was no deeper down
Than me.

And when they thought
That I was gone forever
That I was all the way
In hell
I got right back into my body
And came back out
And rang my bell.

No matter how
They try to harm me now
No matter where
They lay me in the grave
No matter what injustices they do
I've seen the root
Of all that believe.

I've seen the room
Where life and death are made
And I have known
The secret forge of war
I even saw the womb
That all things come from
For I got down so far!

But when they thought
That I was gone forever
That I was all the way
In hell
I got right back into my body
And came back out
And rang my bell.[45]

Most Christian commentary on the Book of Jonah has been concerned to draw out certain points of comparison between Jonah's experience and the life, death, and resurrection of Christ. But, on occasion, the drama of Jonah's life has been regarded simply as an image – albeit a rather heightened image – of what life is like for all of us in this world. The Anglican Bishop of Salisbury, for example, John Jewel, writing towards the end of the sixteenth century, draws the reader's attention, first of all, to the paradoxical nature of Jonah's

45. *The Collected Poems of Thomas Merton* (New York 1977) pp. 669-70.

39

experience inside the whale's belly: '[T]he place was very dark: the waves beat on every side: he was drowned yet touched no water; he was swallowed up, yet not consumed … the tempest was death, yet he died not, but lived in the midst of death; he could not see, he could not hear, he knew not to whom he might call for help'.[46] Then, Bishop Jewel adds: 'Let us mark well this story: it is a true pattern of our estate, and sheweth what our Life is in this world'.[47]

In similar vein, the third century martyr and bishop, Methodius, in a fragment on Jonah, states that 'the ship in which [Jonah] embarked, and which was tempest-tossed, is this brief and hard life in the present time … And the storm and the tempests which beat against us are the temptations of this life … And being swallowed by the whale signifies our inevitable removal by time. For the belly in which Jonah, when he was swallowed, was concealed, is the all-receiving earth, which receives all things which are consumed by time.'[48]

46. John Jewel, *A Treatise of the Holy Scriptures* (1570), cited in Jack M. Sasson, *Jonah* (New York 1990) p. 65.

47. *Ibid.*, p. 65.

48. Methodius, 'On the History of Jonah', in *The Ante-Nicene Fathers*, Vol VI (Fathers of the Third Century) p. 378. For yet another reflection in this vein, see the ancient Jewish text called *The Zoar*, in which a certain Rabbi Abba remarks that 'In the story of Jonah we have a representation of the whole of a man's career in this world … Man, then, is in this world as in a ship that is traversing the great ocean and is like to be broken.' Cited in James Limburg, *Jonah: A Commentary*, p. 108.

But what of the *Christian* experience? What of life in Christ? As believers can we not expect to enjoy the security, the serenity, of faith? Are we not protected from 'the shocks that flesh is heir to', and from the storms of fate? We *are* protected, I would say, and we are *not* protected. Life in Christ – true religion – does not take the cross out of our lives. It does not render us immune to great suffering or misfortune. And yet, no matter how relentless or terrible the storm might appear, because Christ himself is at the heart of the storm, and because, as our Redeemer, he lives within us, and we in him, we have no reason to be afraid.

Here I think it is necessary to make a distinction between what John Macmurray has called illusory religion and real religion: 'The maxim of illusory religion runs: "Fear not; trust in God and he will see that none of the things you fear will happen to you"; that of real religion, on the contrary, is "Fear not; the things that you are afraid of are quite likely to happen to you, but they are nothing to be afraid of"!'[49]

Of course, it is also true, thank God, that we are given wonderful gifts in this life, gifts of family-life and friendship, of individual talents and vocation, gifts of adventure and discovery, of places to visit and revisit, and also – not to be forgotten – gifts of happiness and success in our work. But not

49. John Macmurray, *Persons in Relation* (London 1970) p. 171.

all of us – it has to be said – are blessed with these gifts. And none of us can hold on to them forever. For whether you are rich or poor, believer or non-believer, busy business executive or contemplative religious, whether you are young or old, handsome or ugly, weak or strong, life in this world – given its suddenness and mystery, its beauty and horror, its puzzle, uncertainty and risk – *is* a bewilderment.[50]

One of the things I admire about the Trappist monk, Thomas Merton, is that he faced this truth head on. And it was to Jonah that he looked, in his writings, in order to express the paradox and bewilderment of his own life, his own vocation. Merton felt that his life as a monk, in particular, had been sealed with the sign of Jonah, that it had been somehow burned into the roots of his being. And why? Because he found himself, as he puts it, 'travelling toward my destiny in the belly of a paradox'.[51] Like Jonah, he had been ordered to go to his own Nineveh. But Merton admits: 'I found myself with an almost uncontrollable desire to go in the opposite direction. God pointed one way and all my "ideals" pointed

---

50. Cardinal Newman, although utterly convinced of the existence of God, writes in *Apologia Pro Vita Sua*, of the 'heart-piercing, reason-bewildering fact' of the apparent absence of God in the drama of human history. 'I look out of myself into the world of men,' he writes, 'and there I see a sight that fills me with unspeakable distress. The world seems simply to give the lie to that great truth, of which my whole being is so full.' (Oxford 1967) pp. 216-17.
51. Thomas Merton, *The Sign of Jonas* (New York 1953) p. 11.

in the other.'[52] But then Merton adds: 'It was when Jonas was travelling as fast as he could away from Nineveh, toward Tharsis, that he was thrown overboard, and swallowed by a whale who took him where God wanted him to go.'[53]

So the moment of actual failure and breakdown – the experience of bewilderment in our lives – can be the moment of *breakthrough*, the moment when God's grace finally shakes down all our defences. And then, to our amazement, from out of the belly of failure, from out of the death of false dreams and false ideals, and even from the jaws of a living hell, we can begin to experience the grace of resurrection.

For a certain number of Christian contemplatives, this experience of the dark night of transformation assumes a truly dramatic form. The Spanish mystic, St John of the Cross, for example, speaks of it as nothing less than a kind of *divinisation*.[54] Clearly, for him, something far more profound than a simple moral change or conversion is involved. He writes: 'the soul … feels that it is melting away and being undone by a cruel spiritual death; it feels as if it were being swallowed by a beast and being digested in the dark belly, and it suffers an anguish comparable to Jonas's when in the belly of the

52. *Ibid.*, p. 10.

53. *Ibid.*, pp. 10-11.

54. See 'The Dark Night', Bk 2, Ch 6, The *Collected Works of St John of the Cross,* trans. K. Kavanaugh and O. Rodriguez (Washington 1973) p. 337.

whale.'[55] But then John concludes: 'It is fitting that the soul be in this sepulchre of dark death in order that it attain the spiritual resurrection for which it hopes.'[56] God's intention throughout this process, John explains, is not in any way to punish the soul. He writes: 'The hand of God does not press down or weigh upon the soul, but only touches it; and this mercifully, for God's aim is to grant it favours and not chastise it.'[57]

To conclude this second part of the book, I would like to draw attention to a poem or a hymn read first by Father Mapple in *Moby Dick*. It is voiced for Jonah. But I think, perhaps, I can say that at some level, or in some way, it speaks for all of us:

> The ribs and terrors in the whale,
> Arched over me a dismal gloom,
> While all God's sun-lit waves rolled by,
> And left me deepening down to doom.
>
> I saw the opening maw of hell,
> With endless pains and sorrows there;
> Which none but they that feel can tell –
> Oh, I was plunging to despair.

55. *Ibid.*
56. *Ibid.*
57. *Ibid.*, Bk 2, Ch 5, p. 337.

In black distress, I called my God,
When I could scarce believe him mine,
He bowed his ear to my complaints –
No more the whale did me confine.

With speed he flew to my relief,
As on a radiant dolphin borne;
Awful, yet bright, as lightening shone
The face of my Deliverer God.

My song forever shall record
That terrible, that joyful hour;
I give the glory to my God,
His all the mercy and the power.[58]

---

58. *Moby Dick*, pp. 46-7.

PART THREE

Compassion without Limit:
The Lesson of the Wondrous Plant

So Jonah is belched out onto dry land. But the story does not end there. 'The word of the LORD,' we read, 'came to Jonah a second time: "Set out for the great city of Nineveh, and announce to it the message I will tell you".' (Jonah 3:1-2) This time, Jonah actually obeyed. According to the description of our hero by Father Mapple in *Moby Dick*: 'Jonah, bruised and beaten – his ears, like two sea-shells still multitudinously murmuring of the ocean',[59] set out for the great city.

In all the whirligig of events which follow (an extraordinary drama in which our hero fails once more to emerge in an impressive light) there is one incident, one stunning image of beauty and repose, that is worth noting: the incident of the gourd plant. Jonah, in a mood of depression and self-pity, had sought out a refuge from the heat of the day. But, according to the biblical text, 'the LORD God provided a gourd plant, that grew up over Jonah's head, giving shade that relieved him of any discomfort'. Needless to say, as the text indicates, 'Jonah was very happy over the plant.' (Jonah 4:6)

The image of Jonah the prophet, stretched-out, blissful under his gourd plant, has often been represented in Christian art, and also in the art of Islam.[60] For as powerfully and convinc-

59. *Ibid.*, p. 53.

60. The Jonah image on p. 47 is taken from a medieval Islamic text entitled *History of the World* by Rashid al-Din (707 AH, 1307 AD). Jonah (or Yūnus) is the only one of the major and minor prophets who is cited by his own name in the Koran. Mohammed does not hesitate, in fact, to number him

ingly as any other image, it offered, or seemed to offer to believers, a glimpse of the true ease of self that would be theirs in the kingdom of God. In Jonah's case, however, the moment of bliss was short-lived. At dawn the next morning, by God's command, Jonah's wondrous plant was attacked by a worm and the plant withered. Jonah was furious. But God said unto Jonah: 'Do you think you have reason to be angry over this plant?' And Jonah answered: 'Yes! I do have reason to be angry – angry enough to die!' (Jonah 4: 9)

Jonah's rage against God, when he realises that his plant is ruined, has been depicted on occasion by Jewish artists over the centuries. But Christian painters and sculptors have, for some reason, shown a marked reluctance to paint or sculpt the anger of the prophet. There is, however, one striking exception. On the great wall of the Sistine Chapel, Jonah is represented as a young man in a state of sudden and uncontainable fury. He is shown seated alongside his withered plant, and is by far the largest figure in the chapel. In fact, so dynamic and so enormous is the painted image of the prophet, it can be said to dominate the Last Judgment fresco of Michelangelo.[61]

among the apostles of God. See 'Yūnus, the prophet Jonah' in *Shorter Encyclopaedia of Islam*, eds. H. A. R. Gibb and J. H. Kramers (Leiden 1974) pp. 645-46. See also 'Jonah in Islam', in James Limburg, *Jonah: A Commentary* (Louisville, Kentucky 1993) pp. 113-18.

61. When it was first seen, the great fresco of Jonah occasioned awe among Michelangelo's contemporary artists. Vasari expressed the view of many

Reading through the Book of Jonah, we soon come to realise that God speaks to us, not only through his word, but also through our own confused emotions. Jonah's relationship with God, at least to some significant degree, consists in a series of different states of feeling, all of which have been provoked by different circumstances: emotions of guilt, for example, or of fear or of joy.

The nearer God comes to an individual man or woman, we might expect that person to experience a kind of sustained bliss, or at least some kind of intense emotional rapture. But such 'glorious bewilderment' is not, in fact, all that common in the Christian life. St Teresa of Avila, it is true, and with her a considerable number of other saints and mystics, refer on occasion to a stage in prayer in which the soul is so bewildered by the joy of love, it hardly knows what to say or do. '[I]t cannot tell,' Teresa writes, 'whether to speak or be silent, whether to laugh or weep. It is a glorious bewilderment, a heavenly madness, in which true wisdom is acquired, and to the soul a fulfilment most full of delight.'[62] But such a state of rapture, if it occurs at all, occurs generally at a very advanced stage in the spiritual life.

when he wrote: 'Who could not admire and be struck with amazement by the awesome appearance (*la terribiltà*) of Jonah, the last figure in the chapel?' See Giorgio Vasari, *Le vite dei piu eccellenti pittori, scultori e architetti* (Florence 1891) p. 531.
62. *The Life of St Teresa of Avila by Herself*, Ch 16, trans. J. M. Cohen (London 1957) p. 112.

What happens, in contrast, in the early or beginning stages, is that the warmth of God's love, being so close, stirs up in our hearts all kinds of buried hurts and resentments and weaknesses. St John of the Cross – Teresa's fellow Carmelite and mystic – explains: 'All the soul's infirmities are brought to light; they are set before its eyes to be felt and healed. Now with the light and heat of the divine fire, it sees and feels those weaknesses and miseries which previously resided within it, hidden and unfelt.'[63] In practice, therefore, at least in the early stages, instead of beaming with a new-found spirituality, we very quickly begin to appear like a damp log of wood which has had fire applied to it. For, paradoxically, before we ourselves can catch fire with love, we begin first, according to St John of the Cross, to 'sweat and smoke and sputter'![64]

Often, in fact, it is in the midst of our emotional and passionate

63. See 'The Living Flame of Love', Stanza 1:21-2, in *The Collected Works of St John of the Cross,* trans. K. Kavanaugh and O. Rodriguez (Washington 1973) p. 587.

64. *Ibid.,* Stanza 1, 22, p. 587. Worth noting here, in passing, is a moment of profound emotional distress and bewilderment in the life of St John of the Cross. He had managed to escape from Toledo, where he had been imprisoned and tortured by his own brethren, only to find himself stranded in a place (Andalucia) where he was quite miserable. 'I was swallowed by that whale,' he exclaimed in a letter to a friend, 'and cast up in this strange harbour!' See Letter to M. Catalina de Jesus, July 6, 1581, in *The Complete Works of Saint John of the Cross,* Vol III, trans. E. A. Peers (Wheathampstead 1974) p. 241.

lives, rather than on some exalted spiritual sphere, that God speaks to us, and speaks with great authority. This surprising truth – this Jonah truth – is expressed not only in the work of St John of the Cross, but also in the work of the eighteenth-century Jesuit author, Jean-Pierre de Caussade. Addressing those among us, whose notion of spirituality and spiritual perfection borders on the abstract and the other-worldly, he declares: 'You seek perfection, and it lies in everything that happens to you. Your suffering, your actions, your impulses, are the mysteries under which God reveals himself to you. But he will never disclose himself in the shape of that exalted image to which you so vainly cling.'[65]

Geoffrey T. Bull, commenting on the destruction of Jonah's wondrous plant, imagines God saying to Jonah in rhyme, or in a sort of rhyme: 'When it happened, you went all to pieces. / You shouted me down with your crude exegesis!'[66] The rhyme, of course, is somewhat forced, but the statement is not, I think, inaccurate. For there was something strange from the beginning about Jonah's way of thinking. After all, he was a chosen prophet of Yahweh. And yet, one moment we see him in disobedience, and the next moment in despair.

65. See *The Sacrament of the Present Moment* [*L'Abandon à la Providence Divine*] trans. K. Muggeridge (London 1981) p. 35. This version of De Caussade's work – a reconstitution of the original text based on modern scholarship – was not published in France until 1966.
66. Geoffrey T. Bull, *The City and the Sign: An Interpretation of the Book of Jonah* (London 1970) p. 153.

What was Jonah's problem? What was wrong with his 'exegesis'?

As we begin to understand the message of the Book of Jonah, one thing becomes clear: the prophet's disobedience and despair were merely symptoms of a deeper problem: Jonah, in fact, was a religious bigot. He was a man of strong will but of narrow intelligence, a staunchly religious man, who simply could not bear the idea that Yahweh might want to extend his kindness to people who were not members of his own religion, and especially if those people were living in great sin like the people of Nineveh. So when Jonah received the command from Yahweh to preach 'against the city', he realised right from the beginning that God's threat of punishment was not serious; or rather it *was* serious, but only in the sense of being the expression of a merciful will or desire to call all people to repent, and seek forgiveness. The dilemma of Jonah, at this point in the story, finds very clear expression in Francis Quarles' seventeenth poem concerning the prophet. Quarles places on Jonah's lips these four revealing lines:

> I know my God is gentle, and enclinde
> To tender mercy, apt to change his minde
> Upon the least repentance: Then shall I
> Be deem'd as false, and shame my Prophesie.[67]

---

67. 'A Feast for Wormes', p. 10.

Three centuries later, Robert Frost wrote a poem or a verse-drama concerning Jonah entitled 'A Masque of Mercy'. Asked about the poem in an interview, Frost remarked: 'I noticed that the first time in the world's history when mercy is entirely the subject is in Jonah ... Jonah is told to go and prophesy against the city – and he *knows* that God will let him down. He can't trust God to be unmerciful. You can trust God to be anything but unmerciful. So he ran away and – and got into a whale. That's the point of that and nobody notices it. They miss it.'[68]

Frost's sharp and wry comment is, of course, entirely accurate. For what Jonah guessed from the start – and the idea irritated him deeply – was that Yahweh would probably choose, in the end, not to punish any of the people of Nineveh. And, in that event, he, Jonah, the chosen prophet of doom, after all his preaching, would appear like a false prophet or a complete fool. So Jonah ran away from God, not because he was afraid of God nor because he objected to being a prophet as such, but because of a religious obsession, a mistaken belief about the exclusivity of his own faith, a prej-

68. 'Robert Frost', in *Writers at Work: The Paris Review Interviews*, ed. K. Dick (Harmondsworth 1968) p. 88. One of the protagonists in Frost's verse-drama says to Jonah: 'That book of yours in the Old Testament / Is the first place in literature, I think, / Where Mercy is explicitly the subject. / I say you should be proud of having beaten / The Gospels to it.' See 'A Masque of Mercy' in *The Poetry of Robert Frost*, ed. E. C. Lathem (New York 1975) p. 508.

udice, a 'crude exegesis' to which, in spite of everything he knew, he clung tenaciously.

The message of the Book of Jonah is that God, the living God, is the God of all people and is a God of compassion. In fact, in the opinion of Martin Luther, this tiny book is nothing less than 'a wonderful sign of God's goodness to all the world'.[69] 'Notice,' Luther writes, 'the wonderful attractiveness of the Divine Majesty, how he handled and played with foolish, angry Jonah ... This is the gentle, fatherly way to handle sinners ... Notice how he winks at, how he quarrels with, Jonah's grumbling so that Jonah might ... stop being angry.'[70] As for Jonah himself, Luther makes an observation about the man I have not seen elsewhere, and it is worth noting: Jonah, he writes, is 'a queer and odd saint who is angry because of God's mercy for sinners, begrudging them all benefits and wishing them all evil ... And yet he is God's dear child. He chats so uninhibitedly with God as though he were not in the least afraid of him – as indeed he is not; he confides in him as in a father.'[71]

The full text of the Book of Jonah has been read, since ancient times, in Jewish communities across the world on the feast of

---

69. Martin Luther, 'Lecture on Jonah: The German Text, 1526', p. 36.
70. Luther, 'Lecture on Jonah: The Latin Text, 1525', pp. 28-9.
71. Luther, 'Lecture on Jonah: The German Text', p. 92.

Yom Kippur, the Day of Atonement.[72] And, in the Reform Synagogues of Great Britain, after the close of the Torah Service on that day, the following prayer is recited:

> Lord, you are revealed in the story of Jonah, and we relate its meaning to ourselves; for Nineveh is the repentant world, and we are Israel, its unwilling prophet. You have chosen us to know You and to love You, and this knowledge is our glory, and this love is our burden … such knowledge is too wonderful for us. By it you reveal our kinship to friend and foe, our duty to those who love us, and to those who hate us; our task in a world where everything and everyone is Your work. If we are not for others, we are not for Israel. It is for us to bring the prisoner freedom, to give the homeless refuge, and the starving food. It is for us to sow the seed of friendship on unfriendly soil, to reconcile enemies, and bring redemption to our oppressors … Your command is beyond all calculation.[73]

The Book of Jonah ends with a question. It is a question put to Jonah by God in response to the prophet's bitter complaint about the withering of his gourd plant: 'Then the LORD said,

---

72. On Holy Saturday, in the Greek Orthodox Liturgy, the entire Book of Jonah is read. On the same day, in the Roman Catholic Liturgy, chapter three of the Book of Jonah was read until Vatican II.

73. 'Yom Kippur Afternoon Service' in *Forms of Prayer for Jewish Worship*, Vol III, *Prayers for the High Holidays* (London 1985) p. 551.

"You are concerned over the plant which cost you no labour and which you did not raise; it came up in one night and in one night it perished. And should I not be concerned over Nineveh, the great city, in which there are more than a hundred and twenty thousand persons who cannot distinguish their right hand from their left, not to mention the many cattle?"' (Jonah 4:10-11)

The question, finding no answer from Jonah, has – if I'm not mistaken – a strange and sudden impact on those of us who, up to now, have been following the story. For, in the absence of any further word from God or from his prophet, and with, in fact, the immediate and complete disappearance of Jonah from the scene, it is as if the question put to Jonah about prejudice and compassion is now, all of a sudden, and with a quite remarkable force and authority, directed at ourselves, the readers. We are no longer simply spectators of the Jonah story, but active participants. Each one of us must now respond to the challenge of God's Word, and to the direct call for forgiveness. Here, on the open page in front of us – in the utter silence after the question – we are being offered the surprising freedom and opportunity to write out for ourselves, as it were, the final paragraph of the Book of Jonah.

But what of the prophet himself? We are told nothing at all, in the text, about Jonah's response to God's question. So what are we to make of this gap at the end, this mysterious silence?

Does it indicate, perhaps, a sullen anger on the part of Jonah? Has the unhappy prophet sunk back again into a deep depression? Or has the extravagant kindness of God – the word of compassion – somehow finally silenced the voice of prejudice in the heart of Jonah? In all of the discussion surrounding this matter, over the centuries, I am glad to say a considerable number of commentators, both Jewish and Christian, suggest a positive ending. Thus, in a medieval Jewish homily, for example, we read: 'At that very moment, [Jonah] fell flat on his face saying, "Direct your world according to the attribute of mercy, as it is written, *Mercy and forgiveness belong to the Lord our God".'*[74]

The Book of Jonah has been called, accurately enough, a 'parable of mercy'. It is a work which contains a deeply serious and important message. And yet there is a strain of comedy in the story, a use of burlesque and parody that cannot be ignored. For the work is also a masterpiece of irony, a satire even, in which, scene after scene, the harsh tribalism and religious prejudice of stiff-necked people like Jonah, are directly challenged and also gently mocked.[75] Take the scene on

---

74. *Midrash Yona*, cited in Sasson, p. 320. The quotation in italics is from the Book of Daniel, 9:9.
75. Gently mocked as well, I suspect, are those readers who insist, in our own day, on regarding the text as a literal history, refusing to come to terms not only with the work's literary form but also with its strange mythic extravagance and playfulness.

board ship, for example. While the storm is at its height, where is Jonah? He is down in the ship's hold, fast asleep. But meanwhile, up above on deck, 'the mariners', we're told, 'became frightened, and each one cried to his god'. (Jonah 1:5) So, while the prophet dozes, the sailors – all of them gentiles, and all of them apparently from different religions – are trying to hold on deck a sort of ecumenical prayer service!

No less impressive, of course, is the behaviour of the wicked citizens of Nineveh. For, after hearing only one sentence from the prophet, they repent, all of them. And they undertake a great fast, and put on sack-cloth, and begin to 'call loudly to God'. (Jonah 3:8) The contrast between the Ninevites' spirit of obedience and the disobedience of the Israelite Jonah, is further underlined by one sharp, comic detail. We're told that even the animals in Nineveh, all the countless thousands of them, as a sign of repentance, put on sack-cloth!

I cannot resist drawing attention here, in paranthesis, to a short text from the ancient *Midrash Jonah*. A certain Rabbi ben Chalaftha, no doubt somewhat irritated by the implications of the above story, is quoted as saying that the Ninevites' repentance was, in fact, a complete fraud. He suggests – and the idea is almost as comic as it is outrageous – that the Ninevites practiced a form of emotional blackmail on God. 'What did they do?' he asks, 'They placed calves inside their houses and their mothers outside, so that the calves cried and howled inside, and the cows outside. The people said to the Holy One, blessed be he! If you do not have mercy on us, we will not have mercy on these!'[76] The imagination behind this unusual passage has at least one redeeming feature: God is understood as someone who could not bear to witness for a moment the torture and distress of suffering creatures. But, for the rest, the passage is so wilful and so bizarre, I sometimes wonder if, perhaps, it was written tongue-in-cheek by its author, and if it represents, therefore, in the light of the Jonah story, a kind of deliberate self-parody.

In the Book of Jonah itself, by choosing to employ different types of humour, Jonah's author not only 'delights his readers', as Hans Walter Wolff has observed, 'but also makes it easier for them to perceive God's loving laughter over narrow-minded piety'.[77] Clearly, therefore, the humour in the work is no ornament. In fact, one can say, it forms part of the book's core-revelation. For what is at issue in Jonah, from start to finish, is the transcendent mystery of God's freedom and God's love. And, after reading through the book of Jonah a number of times, one begins to sense that, at the heart of that freedom and that love, there is an unimaginable joy.

Of course, our own minds and hearts are more like Jonah's

76. See Auguste Wünsche, *Aus Israels Lehrhallen,* Vol II (Hildesheim 1967), cited in James Limburg, *Jonah: A Commentary*, p. 111.
77. Hans Walter Wolff, *Obediah and Jonah: A Commentary* (Minneapolis 1986) p. 12.

than we care to admit. And that is why like Jonah we need, in the spiritual life, to be shocked and shaken out of certain fixed ways of thinking and feeling. We need to begin to recognise God in places where we would never, perhaps, have suspected his presence before, and not only in the big city or in the places of our enemies, but also in the many seemingly banal and bizarre circumstances of our lives.

But to learn this lesson, really to learn it, we need, like Jonah, to undergo the grace and mystery of bewilderment. Of course, we need many other graces as well – for example, the grace to sit still, the grace to meditate, and the grace and the energy to work for peace and to fight for justice. But, sometimes, it is only in the midst of the 'tempest', in the heart of a storm of circumstances which we can't control, that we come finally to realise something of the wonderful mystery of God, and realise also how far beyond anything we can imagine or hope for are his plans both for ourselves and for the entire world.

People who have never been bewildered in life, or in spiritual life, are not likely to be in close or living contact with transcendent love. This truth is something that the great Jesuit, Jean-Pierre de Caussade, understood very well. There is a short prayer in his most famous work, *Abandonment to Divine Providence*, which has always impressed me. It is a prayer which asks God somehow to initiate us into the strange, necessary knowledge of bewilderment – a prayer that is instinct, therefore, with the wisdom of the Book of Jonah. I can think of no better way of ending a meditation entitled 'A Journey with Jonah: The Spirituality of Bewilderment' than by drawing attention now to this short prayer:

O Divine Love, conceal yourself,
leap over our suffering,
make us obedient!
Arouse us and confuse us.
Shatter all our illusions and plans
so that we lose our way
and see neither path nor light
until we have found you.[78]

---

78. Jean-Pierre de Caussade, *The Sacrament of the Present Moment [L'Abandon à la Providence Divine]* p. 35.

The Book of Jonah

Chapter 1

[1]This is the word of the LORD that came to Jonah, son of Amittai: [2]'Set out for the great city of Nineveh, and preach against it; their wickedness has come up before me.' [3]But Jonah made ready to flee to Tarshish away from the LORD. He went down to Joppa, found a ship going to Tarshish, paid the fare, and went aboard to journey with them to Tarshish, away from the LORD.

[4]The LORD, however, hurled a violent wind upon the sea, and in the furious tempest that arose the ship was on the point of breaking up. [5]Then the mariners became frightened and each one cried to his god. To lighten the ship for themselves, they threw its cargo into the sea. Meanwhile, Jonah had gone down into the hold of the ship, and lay there fast asleep. [6]The captain came to him and said, 'What are you doing asleep? Rise up, call upon your God! Perhaps God will be mindful of us so that we may not perish.'

[7]Then they said to one another, 'Come, let us cast lots to find out on whose account we have met with this misfortune.' So they cast lots, and thus singled out Jonah. [8]'Tell us,' they said, 'what is your business? Where do you come from? What is your country, and to what people do you belong?' [9]'I am a Hebrew,' Jonah answered them; 'I worship the LORD, the God of heaven, who made the sea and the dry land.'

¹⁰Now the men were seized with great fear and said to him, 'How could you do such a thing!' – They knew that he was fleeing from the LORD, because he had told them. – ¹¹'What shall we do with you,' they asked, 'that the sea may quiet down for us?' For the sea was growing more and more turbulent. ¹²Jonah said to them, 'Pick me up and throw me into the sea, that it may quiet down for you; since I know it is because of me that this violent storm has come upon you.'

¹³Still the men rowed hard to regain the land, but they could not, for the sea grew ever more turbulent. ¹⁴Then they cried to the LORD: 'We beseech you, O LORD, let us not perish for taking this man's life; do not charge us with shedding innocent blood, for you, LORD, have done as you saw fit.' ¹⁵Then they took Jonah and threw him into the sea, and the sea's raging abated. ¹⁶Struck with great fear of the LORD, the men offered sacrifice and made vows to him.

Chapter 2

¹But the LORD sent a large fish, that swallowed Jonah; and he remained in the belly of the fish three days and three nights. ²From the belly of the fish Jonah said this prayer to the LORD, his God:

Psalm of Thanksgiving

3 Out of my distress I called to the LORD,
   and he answered me;
   From the midst of the nether world I cried for help,
   and you heard my voice.

4 For you cast me into the deep, into the heart of the sea,
   and the flood enveloped me;
   All your breakers and your billows
   passed over me.

5 Then I said, 'I am banished from your sight!
   yet would I again look upon your holy temple.'

6 The waters swirled about me, threatening my life;
   the abyss enveloped me;
   seaweed clung about my head.

7 Down I went to the roots of the mountains;
   the bars of the nether world
   were closing behind me forever,
   But you brought up my life from the pit,
   O LORD, my God.

8 When my soul fainted within me,
   I remembered the LORD;
   My prayer reached you
   in your holy temple.

9 Those who worship vain idols
   forsake their source of mercy.

10 But I, with resounding praise,
   will sacrifice to you;

What I have vowed I will pay:
    deliverance is from the LORD.

[11]Then the LORD commanded the fish to spew Jonah up upon the shore.

Chapter 3

[1]The word of the LORD came to Jonah a second time: [2]'Set out for the great city of Nineveh, and announce to it the message that I will tell you.' [3]So Jonah made ready and went to Nineveh, according to the LORD's bidding. Now Nineveh was an enormously large city; it took three days to go through it. [4]Jonah began his journey through the city, and had gone but a single day's walk announcing, 'Forty days more and Nineveh shall be destroyed,' [5]when the people of Nineveh believed in God; they proclaimed a fast and all of them, great and small, put on sackcloth.

[6]When the news reached the king of Nineveh, he rose from his throne, laid aside his robe, covered himself with sackcloth, and sat in the ashes. [7]Then he had this proclaimed throughout Nineveh, by decree of the king and his nobles: 'Neither man nor beast, neither cattle nor sheep, shall taste anything; they shall not eat, nor shall they drink water. [8]Man and beast shall be covered with sackcloth and call loudly to God; every man shall turn away from his evil way and from

the violence he has in hand. ⁹Who knows, God may relent and forgive, and withhold his blazing wrath, so that we shall not perish.' ¹⁰When God saw by their actions how they turned from their evil way, he repented of the evil that he had threatened to do to them; he did not carry it out.

Chapter 4

¹But this was greatly displeasing to Jonah, and he became angry. ²'I beseech you, LORD,' he prayed, 'is not this what I said while I was still in my own country? This is why I fled at first to Tarshish. I knew that you are a gracious and merciful God, slow to anger, rich in clemency, loathe to punish. ³And now, LORD, please take my life from me; for it is better for me to die than to live.' ⁴But the LORD asked, 'Have you reason to be angry?'

⁵Jonah then left the city for a place to the east of it, where he built himself a hut and waited under it in the shade, to see what would happen to the city. ⁶And when the LORD God provided a gourd plant, that grew up over Jonah's head, giving shade that relieved him of any discomfort, Jonah was very happy over the plant. ⁷But the next morning at dawn God sent a worm which attacked the plant, so that it withered. ⁸And when the sun arose, God sent a burning east wind; and the sun beat upon Jonah's head till he became

faint. Then he asked for death, saying, 'I would be better off dead than alive.'

9But God said to Jonah, 'Have you reason to be angry over the plant?' 'I have reason to be angry,' Jonah answered, 'angry enough to die.' 10Then the LORD said, 'You are concerned over the plant which cost you no labour and which you did not raise; it came up in one night and in one night it perished. 11And should I not be concerned over Nineveh, the great city, in which there are more than a hundred and twenty thousand persons who cannot distinguish their right hand from their left, not to mention the many cattle?'